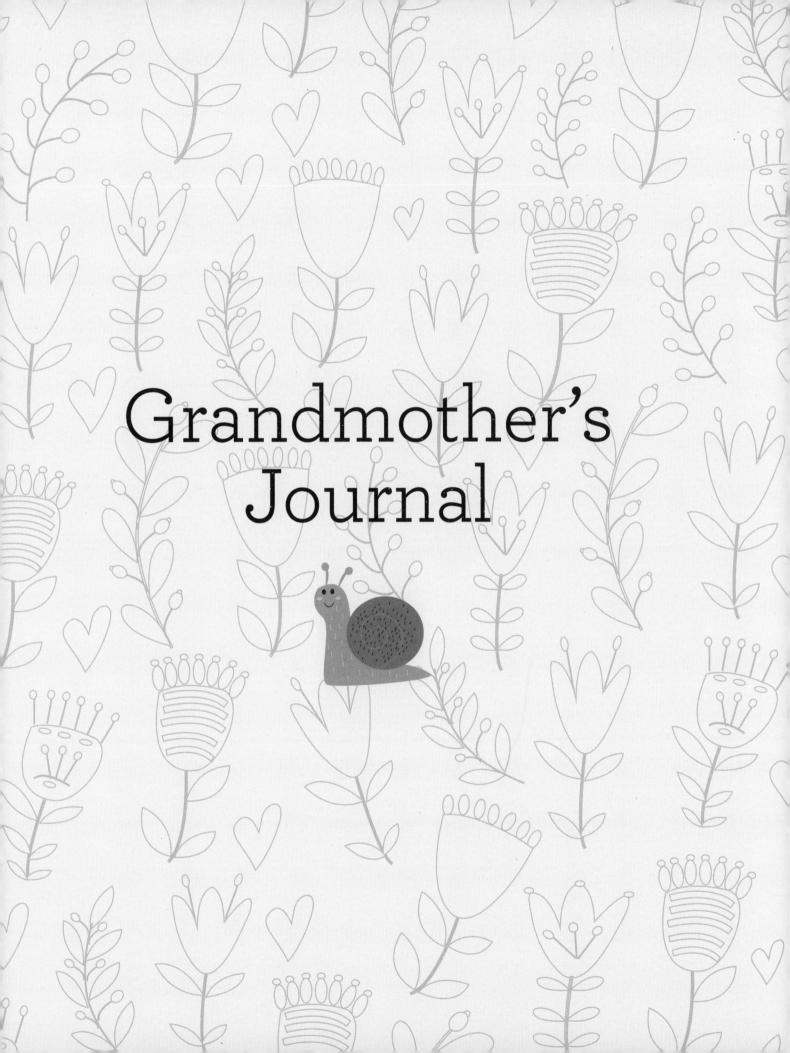

Grandmother's
Journal

Grandmother's Journal

MEMORIES AND KEEPSAKES FOR MY GRANDCHILD

Star Fiore

Bluestreak
BOOKS

Bluestreak

an imprint of Weldon Owen
1045 Sansome Street, San Francisco, CA 94111
www.weldonowen.com
Weldon Owen is a division of Bonnier Publishing USA

Library of Congress Cataloging in Publication data is available.

Printed in China

ISBN-13: 9781681881782

First Printed in 2017
2017 2018 2019 2020
10 9 8 7 6 5 4 3 2 1

ILLUSTRATION CREDITS:

© iStockPhoto/shlyonik: 1–3, 13 (owl), 16–17, 21, 28 (bottom), 29 (bottom), 31, 34–35, 44–45, 48–49 (background), 51–55, 62 (bottom), 63 (top), 78–79, 85, 92 (bottom), 93; ©iStockPhoto/mxtama: cover (background), 4–5, 6–7 (background), 10–11 (background), 12, 14–15, 18–20, 22–23, 24–25 (background), 26–27, 28 (top), 29 (top), 30, 32–33, 38–41, 43, 46–47, 50, 56–57, 64–67, 68–69 (background), 72–77, 80–81 (background), 82–84, 86–91, 92 (top), 94–96; ©iStockPhoto/ aleksandarvelasevic: (dingbat) cover, 7, 11, 25, 37, 49, 69, 81; ©iStockPhoto/eduardrobert: 8–9, 13 (branch); ©iStockPhoto/ShadyMaple: 36–37 (background); ©iStockPhoto/lucrta Design: 42; ©iStockPhoto/mashuk: 58–59; ©iStockPhoto/Angel_1978: 60–61; ©iStockPhoto/Nata_Slavetskaya: 62 (top), 63; ©iStockPhoto/PaCondryx: 70–71

Contents

Introduction

A Private Note to Grandkids from the Publisher

We're going to print this note really small, so your grandma can't read it. It's private, only for you.

You already know that grownups were kids once, but have you ever really thought about what your grandmother was like when she was your age? What did she look like on the first day of school? What did she do when she was a teenager? How did she meet your grandfather? Where was she when your mom or dad was born? What was the thing your parent did that made her the proudest... or the maddest, and why?

This journal is her place to tell you the things about herself and your family history that you will want to know one day, even if you don't realize it yet.

And as you grow up, you will treasure this special keepsake, in which your grandmother has shared her stories, dreams, and wisdom—just for you! So even if it seems like a weird gift now, hold onto it, talk to your grandmother about it, ask her to tell you more stories and find pictures you can keep in it, and one day you will be very happy that you did!

My Family Tree

Great-Grandmother

Great-Grandmother

Great-Grandfather

Great-Grandfather

My Grandmother

My Grandfather

My Mother

Me

My Sibling

My Sibling

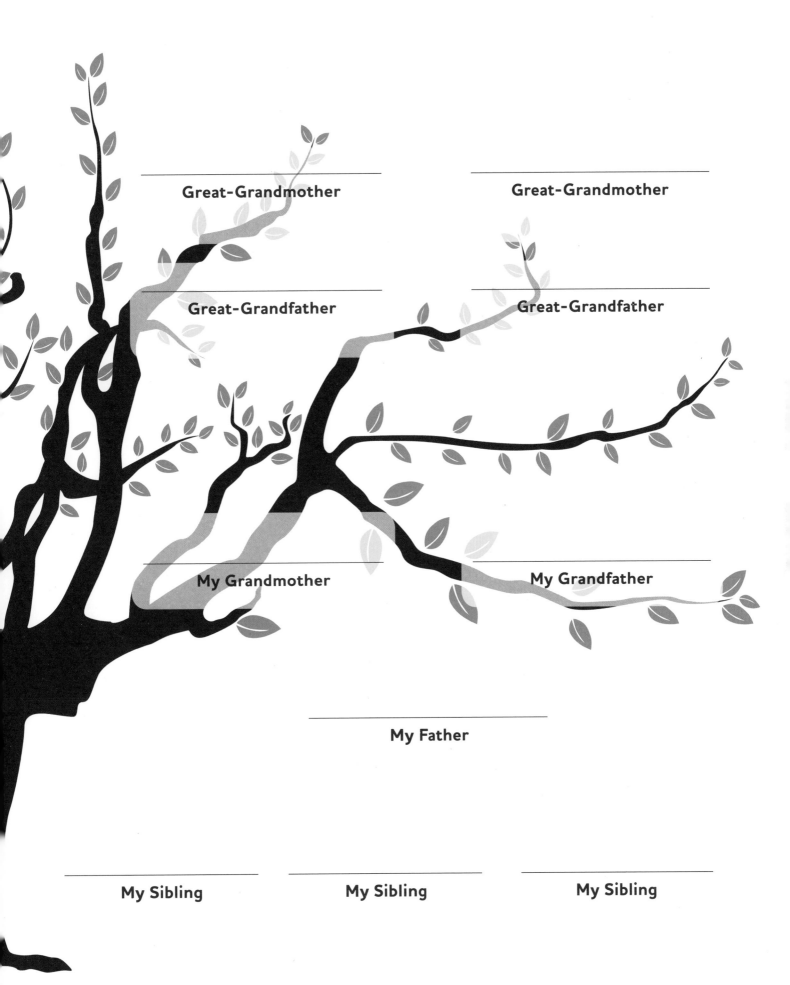

Great-Grandmother

Great-Grandmother

Great-Grandfather

Great-Grandfather

My Grandmother

My Grandfather

My Father

My Sibling

My Sibling

My Sibling

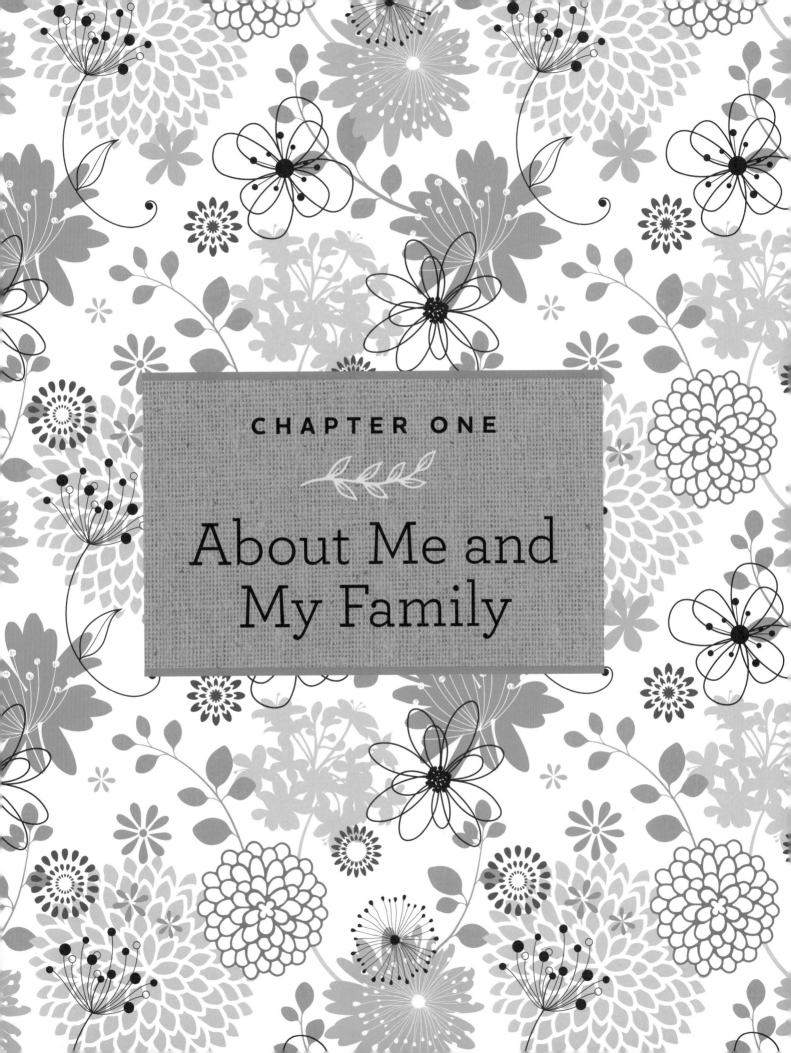

CHAPTER ONE

About Me and My Family

When I Was Born

There is no doubt that it is around the family and the home that all the greatest virtues, the most dominating virtues of human, are created, strengthened and maintained.

—WINSTON S. CHURCHILL

I was born in _____

_____,

which is near _____

My family's address was _____

My birthday is _____

My parents named me (full name) _____

They chose my name because _____

My nickname was _____

THE OTHER MEMBERS OF MY FAMILY

Brothers (dates of birth) _____

Sisters (dates of birth) _____

About My Parents

The future belongs to those who believe in the beauty of their dreams.

—ELEANOR ROOSEVELT

My parents (your great-grandparents!) were named _____

_____ ,

and _____

_____

My mother was born in _____

_____

My father was born in _____

_____

How my parents met _____

_____

My parents earned their living by

Things they liked to do together

Words I would use to describe my mother

Words to describe my father

My mother's education _____

_____

My father's education _____

_____

My mother's interests _____

_____

My father's interests _____

_____

Things our family enjoyed doing together _____

_____

_____

A family vacation we took together _____

_____

_____

A trait (or traits) I got from my mother _____

_____

_____

A trait (or traits) I got from my father _____

_____

_____

A story I want to share about my family when I was growing up _____

_____

_____

_____

_____

_____

_____

About My Grandparents
(Your Great-greats!)

You've got to do your own growing, no matter how tall your grandfather was.

—IRISH PROVERB

My mother's parents were named _____

and _____

They lived in _____

Their other children—my aunts and uncles—were named (include birthdates) _____

They made their living by _____

The things I most remember about them are _____

_____

_____

_____

My father's parents were named _____

_____

and _____

_____

They lived in _____

_____

Their other children—my aunts and uncles—were named (include birthdates) _____

_____

_____

_____

They made their living by _____

_____

_____

The things I most remember about them are _____

_____

_____

_____

About Our Family's Heritage

As you discover what strength you can draw from your community in this world from which it stands apart, look outward as well as inward. Build bridges instead of walls.

—SONIA SOTOMAYOR

My family's nationality is _____

_____

_____

Our ethnic background is _____

_____

_____

My relatives came from these places _____

_____

_____

_____

_____

The origins of our family name are _____

_____

_____

My favorite relative growing up was _____

because _____

_____

_____

_____

Some traditions that we observed from our ethnic heritage were _____

_____

_____

_____

_____

We also followed these religious traditions _____

_____

_____

_____

_____

I remember hearing these stories about our family's history _____

_____

_____

_____

_____

_____

Foods

First we eat, then we do
everything else.

—M.F.K. FISHER

Some of the foods my family liked to eat were _____

_____

_____

_____

Traditional family dishes that we ate were _____

_____

_____

Something I remember well about family meals when I was growing up _____

_____

_____

_____

Our family had these rules about dinner time ⎯⎯⎯⎯⎯⎯⎯⎯⎯⎯⎯

⎯⎯⎯⎯⎯⎯⎯⎯⎯⎯⎯⎯⎯⎯⎯⎯⎯⎯⎯⎯⎯⎯⎯⎯⎯⎯⎯⎯⎯⎯⎯⎯⎯⎯

⎯⎯⎯⎯⎯⎯⎯⎯⎯⎯⎯⎯⎯⎯⎯⎯⎯⎯⎯⎯⎯⎯⎯⎯⎯⎯⎯⎯⎯⎯⎯⎯⎯⎯

My favorite foods as a child were ⎯⎯⎯⎯⎯⎯⎯⎯⎯⎯⎯⎯⎯⎯⎯⎯

⎯⎯⎯⎯⎯⎯⎯⎯⎯⎯⎯⎯⎯⎯⎯⎯⎯⎯⎯⎯⎯⎯⎯⎯⎯⎯⎯⎯⎯⎯⎯⎯⎯⎯

⎯⎯⎯⎯⎯⎯⎯⎯⎯⎯⎯⎯⎯⎯⎯⎯⎯⎯⎯⎯⎯⎯⎯⎯⎯⎯⎯⎯⎯⎯⎯⎯⎯⎯

A food I really did not like was ⎯⎯⎯⎯⎯⎯⎯⎯⎯⎯⎯⎯⎯⎯⎯⎯⎯

⎯⎯⎯⎯⎯⎯⎯⎯⎯⎯⎯⎯⎯⎯⎯⎯⎯⎯⎯⎯⎯⎯⎯⎯⎯⎯⎯⎯⎯⎯⎯⎯⎯⎯

Some dishes we ate on special occasions were ⎯⎯⎯⎯⎯⎯⎯⎯⎯

⎯⎯⎯⎯⎯⎯⎯⎯⎯⎯⎯⎯⎯⎯⎯⎯⎯⎯⎯⎯⎯⎯⎯⎯⎯⎯⎯⎯⎯⎯⎯⎯⎯⎯

⎯⎯⎯⎯⎯⎯⎯⎯⎯⎯⎯⎯⎯⎯⎯⎯⎯⎯⎯⎯⎯⎯⎯⎯⎯⎯⎯⎯⎯⎯⎯⎯⎯⎯

⎯⎯⎯⎯⎯⎯⎯⎯⎯⎯⎯⎯⎯⎯⎯⎯⎯⎯⎯⎯⎯⎯⎯⎯⎯⎯⎯⎯⎯⎯⎯⎯⎯⎯

Foods that my mother (or father) was really good at making ⎯⎯⎯

⎯⎯⎯⎯⎯⎯⎯⎯⎯⎯⎯⎯⎯⎯⎯⎯⎯⎯⎯⎯⎯⎯⎯⎯⎯⎯⎯⎯⎯⎯⎯⎯⎯⎯

⎯⎯⎯⎯⎯⎯⎯⎯⎯⎯⎯⎯⎯⎯⎯⎯⎯⎯⎯⎯⎯⎯⎯⎯⎯⎯⎯⎯⎯⎯⎯⎯⎯⎯

⎯⎯⎯⎯⎯⎯⎯⎯⎯⎯⎯⎯⎯⎯⎯⎯⎯⎯⎯⎯⎯⎯⎯⎯⎯⎯⎯⎯⎯⎯⎯⎯⎯⎯

⎯⎯⎯⎯⎯⎯⎯⎯⎯⎯⎯⎯⎯⎯⎯⎯⎯⎯⎯⎯⎯⎯⎯⎯⎯⎯⎯⎯⎯⎯⎯⎯⎯⎯

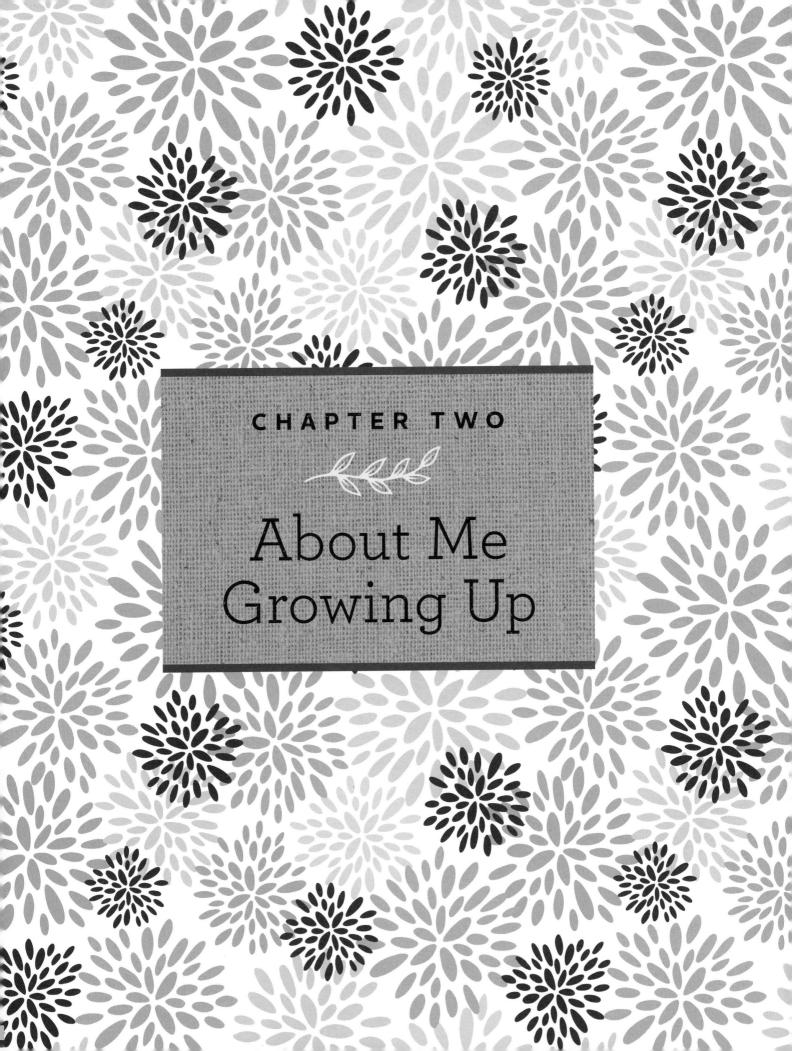

CHAPTER TWO

About Me
Growing Up

About My Home

My childhood home I see again,
And sadden with the view;
And still, as memory crowds my brain,
There's pleasure in it too.

—ABRAHAM LINCOLN

Where I lived when I was a little girl _____

_____

_____

What I remember about my family's home _____

_____

_____

My room was _____

_____

I would describe our neighborhood (include the name if you can) as _____

_____

_____

_____

We had a pet(s) named _____

_____

My best friend(s) were _____

_____

_____

_____

My favorite games _____

_____

_____

My favorite places _____

_____

_____

_____

If I got in trouble, my parents would _____

_____

_____

_____

A memory I want to share with you from when I was a little girl _____

_____

_____

_____

_____

My Elementary Years

My elementary school was called

_____

_____

My favorite teacher was

_____

_____

I got to school by

_____

_____

After school, most days I would

_____

_____

_____

A memory I have from elementary school

_____

_____

_____

_____

_____

_____

My Middle School Years

My middle school was called _____

_____

My favorite teacher was _____

My favorite subjects in school were _____

_____

_____

I got to school by _____

Some of my best friends from middle school were _____

_____

_____

My extracurricular activities and hobbies _____

_____

A memory I have from middle school _____

_____

_____

_____

My High
School

My high school was called

_____

_____

_____

My favorite teacher(s)

_____

_____

_____

My favorite subjects in school were

_____

_____

_____

I got to school by

_____

_____

The things I liked to do after school were

Some of my best friends from high school were

My extracurricular activities and hobbies included

A memory I have from high school

When I Was a Teen

As a teenager you are at the last stage in your life when you will be happy to hear that the phone is for you.

—FRAN LEBOWITZ

My favorite kind of music was _____

_____

_____

I used to listen to it while I was _____

_____

I played (or liked) this instrument _____

_____

How we listened to music when I was a teen _____

_____

Songs that meant a lot to me when I was a teenager _____

_____

_____

_____

Musicians I admired included

Songs or musicians I would like to share with you (and why)

A story about listening to music that I want to share with you

These are a few of my favorite books and authors from when I was young

A story or book that meant a lot to me when I was a kid was

Some books that I hope you will read and enjoy one day

These are a few of my favorite TV shows and movies from when I was young _____

_____

_____

_____

One show or movie that meant a lot to me when I was a kid was _____

_____

A movie or show that I hope we will watch together is _____

_____

I was athletic/not so much. _____

I liked to be outdoors/indoors. _____

In my spare time, I liked to _____

_____

_____

_____

When I was a teenager, most kids would wear _____

_____

_____

_____

My signature outfit or look was _____

_____

_____

I wore my hair _____

_____

My best friend was

We got into trouble when

My social life was

Someone who had a big influence on me was

,

because

Overall, I would describe my my teenage years as

Something I learned as a teenager that I think you might like to know

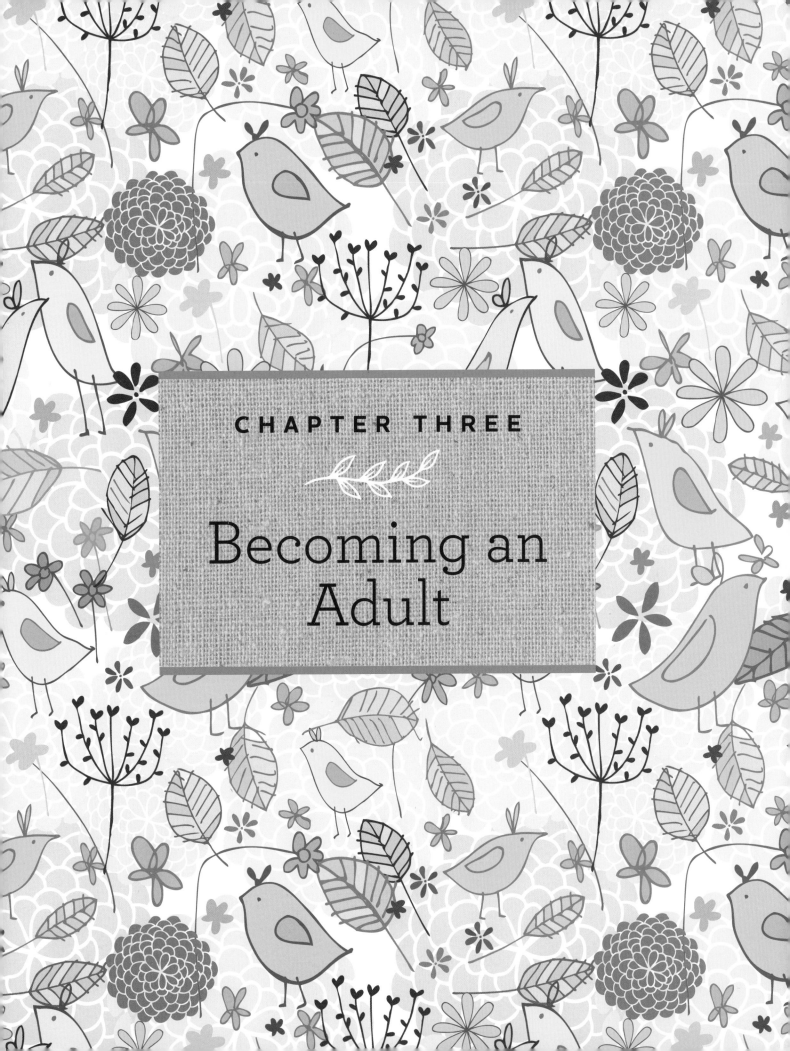

CHAPTER THREE

Becoming an Adult

On My Own

It is always sad when someone leaves home, unless they are simply going around the corner and will return in a few minutes with ice-cream sandwiches.

—LEMONY SNICKET

After high school, I (traveled, went to college, graduate school, the military, work, etc.) _____

_____

_____

_____

I lived _____

_____

I continued school at/went to work at _____

_____

_____

I studied/learned _____

_____

_____

What was important to me back then was _____

_____

_____

_____

_____

My social life was _____

_____

Some of my best memories from those years are _____

_____

_____

_____

My dreams and goals in those years included _____

_____

_____

_____

Something I learned in my early twenties that I want to share with you _____

_____

_____

_____

_____

My Early Career

Life's under no obligation to give us what we expect.

—MARGARET MITCHELL

The first (or most interesting) real job I had was _____

_____

_____

_____

It entailed _____

_____

_____

What I liked about it _____

_____

_____

What I didn't like about it _____

_____

_____

What I learned from my first job that I want to share with you _____

_____

_____

_____

The next step in my career was _____

_____

The things I enjoyed most during that time were _____

_____

_____

_____

And the things I didn't like _____

_____

_____

_____

My dreams at that time were _____

_____

_____

_____

What happened next was _____

_____

_____

_____

Love & Marriage

Being deeply loved by someone gives you strength,
while loving someone deeply gives you courage.

—LAO TZU

I first met your grandfather (where and when)

What first struck me about him was

The story of how we met

We dated for (how long?) _____

_____

Some of the things we did together were _____

_____

_____

_____

_____

When I met his family (or my impressions when I got to know them) _____

_____

_____

_____

_____

The story of how we committed to each other _____

_____

_____

_____

_____

_____

Our wedding took place on (date) _____

at (location) _____

_____

_____

Some of the people in attendance were _____

_____

_____

_____

_____

_____

_____

_____

The thing(s) I will always remember about our wedding _____

_____

_____

_____

_____

_____

_____

Our honeymoon or first big trip after our wedding was to _____

_____

_____

_____

Our first home together was in _____

_____

Our first big purchase was _____

_____

Some of our friends and neighbors when we were first married were _____

_____

Our pet(s) (kinds of pet and names) _____

_____

Some of the things we liked to do in those days were _____

_____

_____

_____

_____

_____

Where I've Lived

The ornament of a house
is the friends who frequent it.

—RALPH WALDO EMERSON

1. ADDRESS _____

_____

_____

When I lived there _____

Best thing about this place _____

_____

_____

Worst thing about this place _____

_____

_____

2. ADDRESS _____

_____

When I lived there _____

Best thing about this place _____

_____

_____

Worst thing about this place _____

_____

3. ADDRESS _____

_____

_____

When I lived there _____

Best thing about this place _____

_____

_____

Worst thing about this place _____

_____

4. ADDRESS _____

_____

_____

When I lived there _____

Best thing about this place _____

_____

_____

Worst thing about this place _____

_____

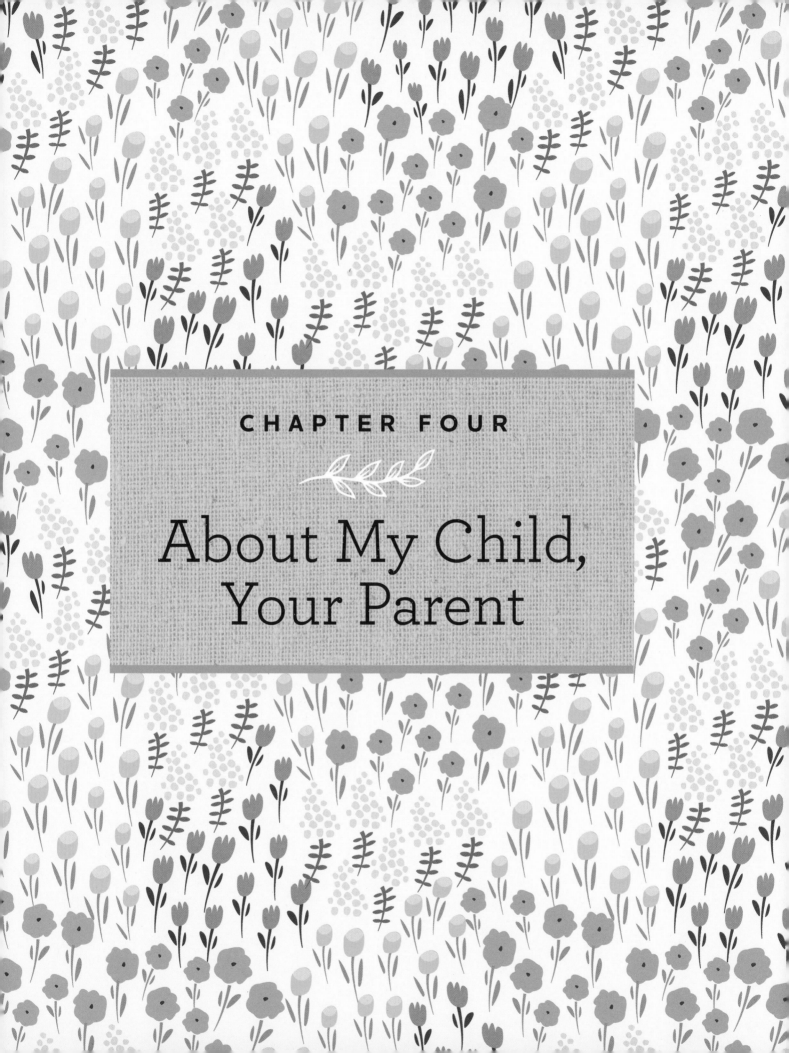

CHAPTER FOUR

About My Child, Your Parent

Your Parent is Born!

We never know the love
of a parent till we become
parents ourselves.

—HENRY WARD BEECHER

When I was pregnant with your parent, we were living in _____

_____

where we earned our livings working at _____

_____

_____ ,

Your parent was born on _____

_____

At this location _____

_____

At this time _____

The story of your parent's birth is _____

_____

_____

_____

We brought the baby home to _____

_____

Here's why we chose your parent's name _____

_____

_____

_____

A story about your parent's first year that I want to share with you is _____

_____

_____

_____

Three words to describe your parent as a baby are _____

_____

A story that we always used to tell about your parent as a baby or toddler was _____

_____

_____

_____

Other things I want to tell you about your parent _____

_____

_____

_____

_____

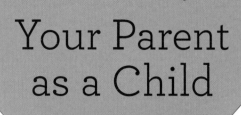

Your Parent as a Child

We can do no great things; only small things with great love.

—MOTHER TERESA

As a child, your parent's favorite activity was

Some of the places we would visit frequently were

Your parent had a sitter or nanny who was (name and description)

Your parent's first school was

Your parent's sibling(s) names and ages (your aunts and uncles) _____

_____

_____

_____

_____

We had a pet that _____

_____

_____

We loved these stories or books _____

_____

_____

_____

_____

_____

Some of your parent's favorite songs _____

_____

_____

_____

_____

Some of your parent's favorite games

Your parent's favorite foods

Least favorite foods

Your parent's favorite things to play with

A funny thing your parent said or did

Something your parent did that made me proud _____

_____

_____

_____

_____

_____

Some of my favorite memories of your parent as a child _____

_____

_____

_____

_____

_____

_____

Notable personality traits your parent had as a child _____

_____

_____

_____

_____

About Your
Parent's Education

Educating the mind without
educating the heart is no education at all.

—ARISTOTLE

Your parent's elementary school was

Your parent got to school by

Your parent's report cards were

Some of your parent's friends during these years were

After school, your parent would

Activities and sports your parent was involved in

Your parent's middle school was

Your parent got to school by

Your parent's report cards were

Some of your parent's friends during these years were

After school, your parent would _____

_____

_____

_____

_____

Activities and sports your parent was involved in _____

_____

_____

_____

_____

Your parent's high school was _____

_____

Your parent got to school by _____

_____

Your parent's report cards were _____

_____

_____

_____

Some of your parent's friends during these years were _____

_____

_____

_____

_____

After school, your parent would _____

_____

_____

_____

_____

_____

Activities and sports your parent was involved in _____

_____

_____

_____

_____

_____

Overall, your parent's strongest subjects in school were _____

_____

_____

_____

_____

About Your Parent As an Older Child

The best way to keep children at home is to make the home atmosphere pleasant, and let the air out of the tires.

—DOROTHY PARKER

As a teenager, your parent's chief interests were _____

_____

_____

_____

_____

I remember your parent liked to wear _____

_____

Your parent's hair was _____

_____

_____

Music your parent listened to

Something your parent did as a teenager that made me proud was

And something that got your parent got into trouble was

Your parent's strongest personality traits as a teenager were

A story I'd like to share with you about when your parent was a teenager is

About Our Family Life

Rejoice with your family in the beautiful land of life.

—ALBERT EINSTEIN

Things we would do together as a family were

_____

_____

_____

_____

_____

Our best family vacation(s) were

_____

_____

_____

_____

During the summer, we would _____

_____

_____

_____

_____

The things I liked about being a parent were _____

_____

_____

_____

_____

_____

_____

Some of the challenges I faced as a parent were _____

_____

_____

_____

_____

_____

About Your Parent as a Young Adult

I have found the best way to
give advice to your children
is to find out what they want and
then advise them to do it.

—HARRY S. TRUMAN

After high school, your parent went to (college, graduate school, the military, work, etc.) _____

_____

The first place your parent lived independently was _____

_____

_____

Your parent's first real job was _____

_____

_____

A memorable visit I had with your parent was _____

_____

_____

_____

_____

When Your Parents Met

Lovers don't finally
meet somewhere.
They're in each other
all along.

—JALAL AL-DIN RUMI

Your parents met at (where and when) _____

_____

_____

The first time I met your other parent was _____

_____

_____

I knew their relationship was going to be special when _____

_____

_____

A story I want to share with you about your parents is _____

_____

_____

_____

_____

About Your Birth

There are only two lasting bequests we can hope to give our children. One of these is roots, the other, wings.

—JOHANN WOLFGANG VON GOETHE

Here's how I found out you were going to be born _____

_____

_____

_____

Where I was when you were born _____

_____

_____

_____

My strongest memories of your birth

How I first met you

This is how your mother was when you were born

This is how your father was when you were born

My first or favorite memories of you as a baby include

CHAPTER FIVE

Family
Traditions

Our Family Gatherings

After a good dinner one can forgive
anybody, even one's own relations.

—OSCAR WILDE

Our family beliefs include

_____

_____

_____

_____

Our important holiday traditions are

_____

_____

_____

_____

The holidays that have always been most special to our family have been _____

_____

_____

_____

_____

_____

A story from a favorite family gathering (where, when, who, and what happened) _____

_____

_____

_____

_____

_____

Family tradition(s) that I hope will continue _____

_____

_____

_____

_____

_____

Our Family Recipes

People who love
to eat are always the
best people.

—JULIA CHILD

Some of our family dishes include _____

_____

_____

_____

My favorite memories of cooking _____

_____

_____

_____

_____

_____

_____

_____

A recipe from your parent's childhood _____

_____

Ingredients _____

_____

_____

_____

_____

_____

_____

Instructions _____

_____

_____

_____

_____

_____

_____

_____

_____

_____

One of my favorite dishes now _____

Ingredients _____

Instructions _____

A recipe I got from my mother or another relative _____

_____

_____

Ingredients _____

_____

_____

_____

_____

_____

_____

Instructions _____

_____

_____

_____

_____

_____

_____

_____

_____

Special Holiday Recipes

HOLIDAY

MAIN COURSE

Ingredients

Instructions

APPETIZER OR SIDE DISH

Ingredients

Instructions

APPETIZER OR SIDE DISH

Ingredients

Instructions

DESSERT _____

Ingredients _____

_____

_____

_____

Instructions _____

_____

_____

_____

_____

HOLIDAY _____

MAIN COURSE _____

Ingredients _____

_____

_____

_____

Instructions _____

_____

_____

_____

APPETIZER OR SIDE DISH

Ingredients

Instructions

DESSERT

Ingredients

Instructions

CHAPTER SIX

About Life and Living

Historic Events in My Lifetime

History doesn't repeat itself, but it does rhyme.

—MARK TWAIN

One of the biggest stories in world news during my lifetime was _____

_____

_____

A world leader I really admired was _____

_____

I remember being truly proud of my country when _____

_____

_____

A big news story that happened in my town was _____

_____

_____

The way I've shown I care about world events is

A funny news story that I can remember happened when

A scientific breakthrough or discovery that improved my life was

A modern convenience that we didn't have when I was a child is

A part of the world that's very different now from when I was young is

Something I've learned about the world that I'd like to share with you is

My Favorites

Some day you will be old enough to start reading fairy tales again.

—C. S. LEWIS

My favorite places, near and far _____

_____

_____

_____

My favorite color(s) _____

_____

My favorite scent(s) _____

_____

My favorite plants and flower(s) _____

_____

_____

_____

My favorite books

My favorite poems

My favorite music

My favorite movies

My favorite plays

Art I love

Other things that make me happy

Me Now

You can have it all.
Just not all at once.

—OPRAH WINFREY

Where I live now _____

_____

What I do most days _____

_____

_____

I work and/or volunteer at _____

_____

My best friends now are _____

_____

_____

_____

_____

The things that I do for fun _____

_____

_____

_____

_____

Things that make me laugh _____

_____

_____

_____

Things that I wish I could change _____

_____

_____

_____

My perfect day _____

_____

_____

_____

Grandma's Wisdom

When you find your path, you must not be afraid. You need to have sufficient courage to make mistakes. Disappointment, defeat, and despair are the tools God uses to show us the way.

—PAULO COELHO

If I could reach back in time and give myself one piece of advice when I was young it would be

Some of the biggest challenges I've faced in my life that I'd like to share with you are

How I've learned to deal with adversity

Some things that have given me comfort in hard times

Things to remember when you're facing a difficult challenge

Recommended reading for good times and bad

Grandma's recipe for happiness

Family Traits I See in You

If you cannot get rid of the family skeleton, you may as well make it dance.

—GEORGE BERNARD SHAW

People in our family you resemble physically include

Your personality reminds me of this relative

Some family traits I wish for you through your life are _____

Family member _____

Trait (include why) _____

_____

_____

_____

_____

Family member _____

Trait (include why) _____

_____

_____

_____

Family member _____

Trait (include why) _____

_____

_____

_____

Family member _____

Trait (include why) _____

_____

_____

_____

My Happiest Memories

The past beats inside me
like a second heart.

—JOHN BANVILLE

My happiest moments with my grandparents _____

_____

_____

_____

My happiest moments with my parents _____

_____

_____

_____

My happiest moments in my married life _____

_____

_____

_____

My happiest moments with your parent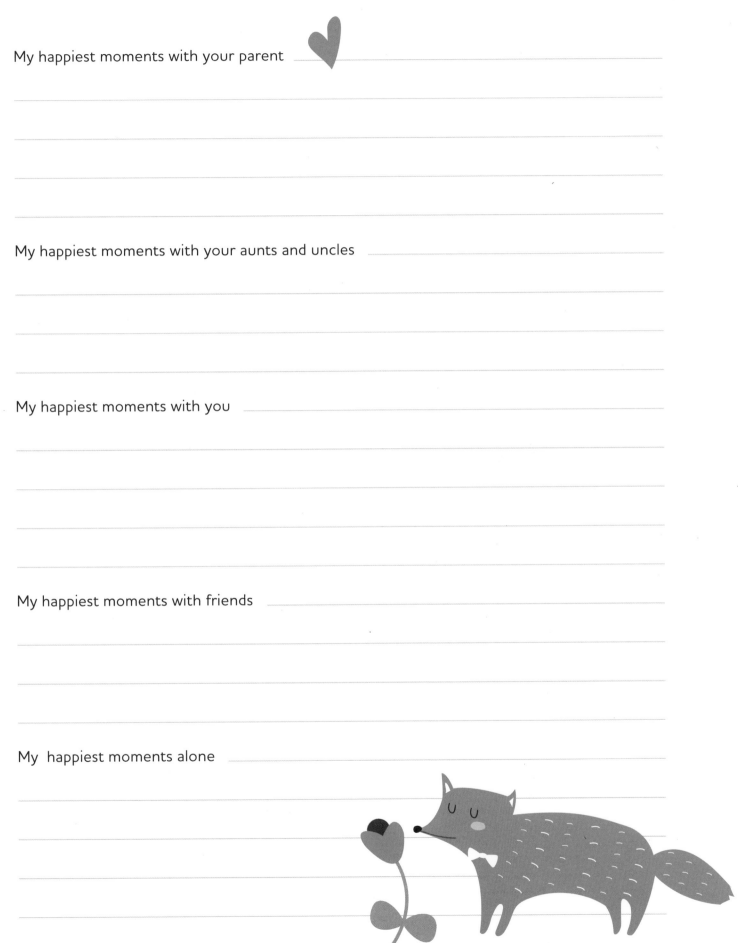

My happiest moments with your aunts and uncles

My happiest moments with you

My happiest moments with friends

My happiest moments alone

My Wishes for You

May you live every day
of your life.

—JONATHAN SWIFT

Some of the things I hope you get to do in your lifetime are _____

_____

_____

_____

_____

Some of the places I hope you get to visit are _____

_____

_____

_____

_____

I hope that in your work life, you are able to _____

_____

_____

_____

I hope you find a partner in life who is _____

_____

_____

_____

_____

I hope that you enjoy doing _____

_____

_____

_____

_____

My biggest dream for you is _____

_____

_____

_____

A Note for You